P9-DTB-316

Arctic Ocean

EUROPE

ASIA

SOUTH KOREA

AFRICA

Pacific

Ocean

Indian

Ocean

AUSTRALIA

ANTARCTICA

NO LONGER PROPERTY OF SEATTLE PUBLIC LIBRARY

Countries of the World

South Korea

Tom Jackson

Leonid A. Petrov and YangMyung Kim, Consultants

NATIONAL GEOGRAPHIC

WASHINGTON, D.C.

Contents

Korea, located in the easternmost part of the Asian continent, prides itself on a unique culture with one of the longest histories in the world. Korea occupies a rather small area of territory, the Korean Peninsula, but at times in the past it controlled vast areas, including southern Manchuria and coastal China.

Today Korea is split into South and North Korea, but in the minds of most Korean people it remains a single nation than cannot be divided. For millennia, they lived as one nation sharing the same culture and a strong sense of national identity. Inspired by deep-rooted pride in themselves as an independent, creative, and determined people, the Korean people brush off the pain and hardship they have suffered during the past century as something temporary and passing. They believe that the nation should—and will—eventually be reunited.

After the devastation of the Korean War (1950–53), Koreans set out to overcome poverty despite facing difficulties such as a lack of natural resources or money for investment. Koreans began to construct, manufacture, and export as fast and as much as they could. Even when the nation was very poor, Korean parents had worked hard at raising and educating their children. Now the highly educated, strongly motivated, and adaptable workforce supports the process of rapid modernization and development. Korea achieved a miracle of economic growth. It made itself one of the most highly industrialized countries in the world. Almost every kind of modern commodity is manufactured in Korea, such as world-renowned telecommunications equipment. The world's tallest skyscraper is now under construction by Korean firms. Korea is also the world's largest ship-building country.

In recent years, the Korean people have also turned their attention toward issues other than economic growth, such as democratization, human rights, and the environment. Political freedom has continued to expand steadily. The well-being of the labor force has become one of the most serious topics in the public arena. More and more people are taking part in preserving the natural ecosystem.

With its dynamism and determination, Korea is taking a leading role with other major countries in developing Asia and improving the well-being of all peoples of the world. Its part in that process will certainly continue to increase.

▲ Craft workers in Gyeongju make papier maché lanterns shaped like strawberries.

YangMyung Kim
Academy of Korean Studies,
Republic of Korea

A Dragon by the Sea

RISING FROM THE SHORE of Jeju Island at the tip of South Korea, or the Republic of Korea, is Yongduam—Dragon Head Rock. According to legend the rock is the remains of a giant dragon that angered a spirit from the nearby volcano Hallasan. The volcano spirit shot the dragon with a magic arrow that turned it to stone. The dragon's body crashed into the sea, and now only its head can be seen until low tide, when its tail also appears.

The South Koreans have many legends about their past. In fact, Dragon Head Rock was formed about two million years ago when Hallasan erupted, spilling streams of lava that became solid as it cooled. Today South Koreans still flock there to enjoy the sun and sea—and perhaps to tell stories about their country.

◀ The dragon's head rises above tourists visiting Yongduam, where they feast on the shellfish for which the island of Jeju is famous.

WHAT'S THE WEATHER LIKE?

South Korea is at the end of a large peninsula. Land surrounded by the ocean on three sides normally has a mild climate, but the South Korean climate is affected by the immense landmass of East Asia to the north. The wind from Siberia blows south over the continent, bringing snow and freezing temperatures to Korea. Only the extreme south escapes the frosts.

In contrast, the summer is hot and wet. More than half of South Korea's annual rain falls between June and August. The map opposite shows the physical features of South Korea. Labels on this map and on similar maps throughout this book identify most of the places pictured in each chapter.

Fast Facts

OFFICIAL NAME: Republic of Korea
FORM OF GOVERNMENT: Republic
CAPITAL: Seoul
POPULATION: 48,846,823
OFFICIAL LANGUAGE: Korean
MONETARY UNIT: Won
AREA: 37,901 square miles (98,190 square kilometers)
BORDERING NATION: North Korea
HIGHEST POINT: Hallasan 6,398 feet (1,950 meters)
LOWEST POINT: East Sea (Sea of Japan) 0 feet (0 meters)
MAJOR MOUNTAIN RANGES: Taebaek Mountains, Sobaek Mountains
MAJOR RIVERS: Han, Kum, Naktong

Average Temperature & Rainfall

Average High/Low Temperatures; Yearly Rainfall
SEOUL:
61° F (16° C) / 44° F (7° C); 54 in (137 cm)
INCHEON:
60° F (15° C) / 46° F (8° C); 42 in (107 cm)
DAEGU:
65° F (19° C) / 46° F (8° C); 39 in (98 cm)
BUSAN:
64° F (18° C) / 50° F (10° C); 58 in (148 cm)
JEJU:
65° F (19° C) / 59° F (15° C); 54 in (137 cm)

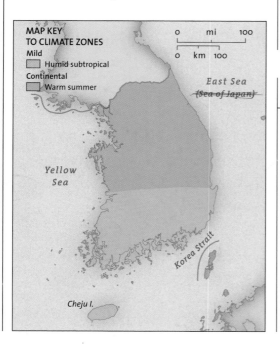

MAP KEY
TO CLIMATE ZONES
Mild
  ▨ Humid subtropical
Continental
  ▨ Warm summer

0   mi   100
0   km   100

East Sea
(Sea of Japan)

Yellow
Sea

Korea Strait

Cheju I.

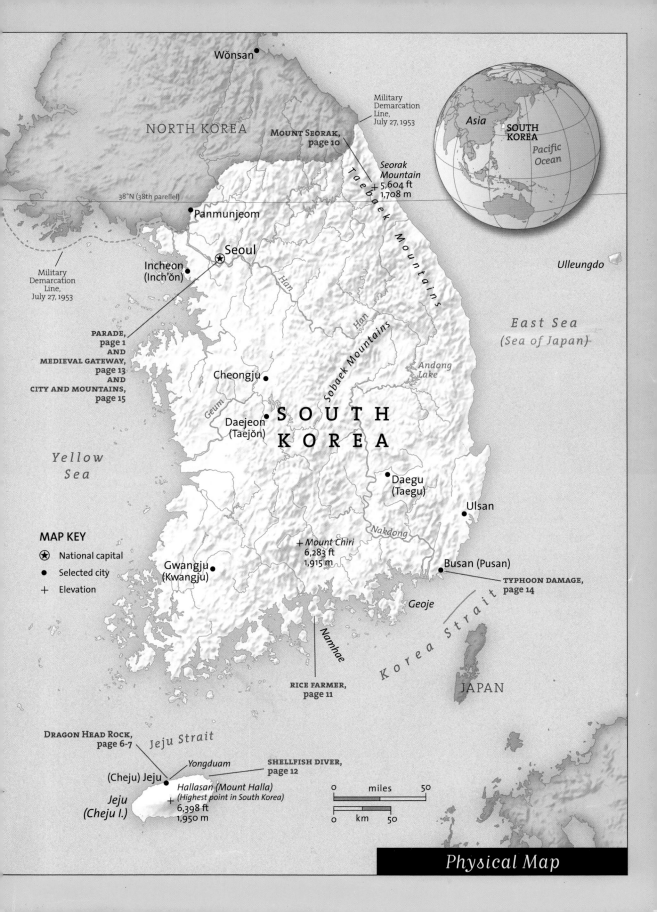

Wŏnsan

NORTH KOREA

Military
Demarcation
Line,
July 27, 1953

MOUNT SEORAK,
page 10

Asia

SOUTH
KOREA

Pacific
Ocean

Seorak
Mountain
+ 5,604 ft
1,708 m

38°N (38th parellel)

Panmunjeom

Seoul

Incheon
(Inch'ŏn)

Military
Demarcation
Line,
July 27, 1953

Han

Han

Ulleungdo

East Sea
(Sea of Japan)

PARADE,
page 1
AND
MEDIEVAL GATEWAY,
page 13
AND
CITY AND MOUNTAINS,
page 15

Cheongju

Daejeon
(Taejŏn)

SOUTH
KOREA

Sobaek Mountains

Taebaek Mountains

Andong
Lake

Geum

Yellow
Sea

Daegu
(Taegu)

Ulsan

MAP KEY

⊛ National capital
● Selected city
+ Elevation

Gwangju
(Kwangju)

+ Mount Chiri
6,283 ft
1,915 m

Nakdong

Busan (Pusan)

TYPHOON DAMAGE,
page 14

Geoje

Namhae

Korea Strait

RICE FARMER,
page 11

JAPAN

DRAGON HEAD ROCK,
page 6-7

Jeju Strait

Yongduam

SHELLFISH DIVER,
page 12

(Cheju) Jeju

Jeju
(Cheju I.)

Hallasan (Mount Halla)
(Highest point in South Korea)
+ 6,398 ft
1,950 m

0   miles   50

0   km   50

Physical Map

▲ The jagged peaks of Mount Seorak tower above village women washing their laundry in a stream before spreading it on the rocks to dry.

Split Down the Middle

The Korean peninsula is roughly 750 miles (1,200 km) long and sticks out of East Asia like a down-turned thumb. To the west is the Yellow Sea, which separates Korea from China. To the east lies the East Sea (which some people call the Sea of Japan).

For most of the last one thousand years, Korea was a single country. At the end of World War II (1939–1945), however, the peninsula was split into two zones by U.S. authorities. The division eventually brought decades of confrontation between North Korea (the Democratic Peoples' Republic of Korea) and South Korea. The border between them, now called the Demilitarized Zone, or DMZ, cuts the peninsula roughly in half.

Rugged and Rocky

South Korea has many mountains, but they are small compared to others around the world. Over millions of years, their peaks have been worn down by the rain and wind. Most summits are under 3,300 feet (1,000 m) high.

According to legend, Korea's divine founder Hwanwoong came down from heaven to the Taebaek Mountains, which run through both North and South Korea. The highest peak, Mount Seorak, is a favorite place of natural beauty for South Koreans and is protected as a national park.

▲ A rice farmer on Namhae Island pushes his family in a rough wooden cart. Rice is South Korea's most important crop.

▼ Terraced rice fields stretch down to the East Sea (Sea of Japan) in Gangwon Province.

The Sobaek Mountains run across the south of the country. Mount Chiri, the tallest peak on the mainland, reaches 6,283 feet (1,915 m). On its southern side is Ssanggyesa Temple, where a monk grew Korea's first tea bushes in about A.D. 828, when he planted tea seeds from China. Today tea is an important crop—and the best tea still comes from Mount Chiri. Korean tea is described as "green" and is made from quickly dried young leaves.

Volcanic Islands

Hallasan on Jeju Island just tops Mount Chiri by 115 feet (35 m).

▲ Jeju Island is famous for its *haenyo*, or divers. These women dive to the seabed to fish for abalone and other shellfish. They are experts at holding their breath—they can stay underwater for over two minutes without any breathing apparatus.

Jeju is the largest of South Korea's islands. There are about 3,000 in all. Many are little more than pieces of uninhabited rock, but dozens of the larger islands are inhabited. South Korea disputes ownership with Japan of a small group of islands, which the Koreans call Dodko, in the East Sea (Sea of Japan).

Draining the Land

Only twenty percent of South Korea's land is suitable for growing crops. The rest is too steep or rocky. Most of the lowlands are in the lower ends of river valleys, which widen as they approach the ocean. South

SO LONG, SEOUL

South Korea is a very crowded country, and Seoul is the most crowded area of all. In 2004 the government decided to build a new capital in the center of the nation. The new city would be less crowded than Seoul, and when government workers moved away Seoul itself would become less cramped and congested. Many businesses would also move out of Seoul, where most of the country's businesses are based, to the new capital. The government decided to build the city in a rural area about 100 miles (160 km) south of Seoul, close to high-speed railway lines and Chungju airport. Construction began in 2007. If all goes according to plan, the new city will become the country's capital in 2030—but before then, it needs a name!

▲ Seoul is such a busy, modern city it has room for just one piece of its old city wall: a 14th-century gateway on a traffic island.

Korea's longest rivers all have their sources in the Taebaek Mountains. The Naktong River—325 miles (523 km) long—drains the Sobaek Mountains. It flows into the Korea Strait, which is often busy with cargo ships heading for Busan or other South Korean ports.

The Han River, South Korea's other main waterway, flows 319 miles (514 km) from east to west. It passes through Seoul before reaching the Yellow Sea at Incheon, the closest deepwater port to Seoul.

HERE COMES MAEMI

Because of its location on the edge of the Pacific Ocean, South Korea often suffers from typhoons—the name given to Pacific hurricanes. Typhoon Maemi first appeared on September 7, 2003. Within days its winds had hit 175 miles per hour (280 kmh). That made it a Category Five storm—the strongest of all. Maemi crossed the ocean south of Japan before turning north and heading straight for South Korea. It looked as though the emergency might have passed, because Maemi's winds had dropped a lot by the time the typhoon hit the coast. But it struck right at high tide. The winds pushed a surge of water over the land, killing 115 people, sinking 282 ships, washing away rice fields, knocking a train off its tracks, and causing four billion dollar's worth of damage.

◀ **Typhoon Maemi reduced these giant container cranes in Busan to a mangled heap of metal.**

Facing the Ocean

Most of the largest cities in South Korea are on or near the coast. Because the country is located on a peninsula, it's impossible to be farther than about 70 miles (112 km) from the sea, even in inland cities.

The eastern coast of South Korea is less built up than the southern or western coasts. The steep coastline there has few natural harbors, while the other coasts are sheltered by offshore islands and have many inlets where ships can drop anchor, although tides can sometimes have a dramatic effect.

At Incheon, for example, the wide mouth of the Han River quickly narrows. Tidal water rushing in to the river piles up on top of itself, creating a very high tide. The difference between high and low tide at

Incheon is one of the largest in the world, at 30 feet (9 m). Ship's captains have to time when they enter or leave the harbor according to the tide.

A Crowded Country

South Korea has 1,256 citizens for every square mile of land (485 per sq km). The United States has 84 people per square mile (32 per sq km). To put it another way, if South Korea was divided into football fields, at least two people would need to share every field—but in the United States each person would have almost seven fields to him or herself!

Because four out of every five South Koreans live in the cities, there are few people living in the countryside. Villages are built close together in sheltered river valleys or in low-lying areas around the coast. Half of South Korea's 40 million city dwellers are crammed into just five cities: Seoul, Busan, Incheon, Daegu, and Daejeon. More and more people are moving to the cities to find work, so the traditions of rural life are starting to disappear.

▼ In South Korea, nowhere is far from the mountains. Even the capital, Seoul, stands in a basin surrounded by rocky ranges.

Pockets
of
Paradise

KOREANS USED TO BELIEVE that tigers were holy animals that represented the mountain gods. They honored tigers for their beauty, fierceness, and strength. The tiger was so important that when South Korea hosted the Olympic Games in 1988, the tiger was chosen as the mascot of the games. Tigers used to roam the Korean peninsula. Today, however, there may be none left at all, although some experts believe a few tigers may still live around the Demilitarized Zone (DMZ), a strip of neutral land between Communist North Korea and South Korea. The belief that tigers have great power is one reason their numbers have fallen. Tiger bones are a valued ingredient in traditional medicines. So hunters have killed the animals to supply the bones.

◀ **A busload of South Koreans have a close encounter with tigers in an amusement park. These tigers were bred in captivity—few, if any, still live in the wild.**

LIFE UNDER PRESSURE

South Korea is only a small country, and there is a huge demand for space. As a result many of the country's natural habitats have been squeezed into smaller and smaller areas, and much of South Korea's wildlife faces an uncertain future. Once, tigers, lynxes, and black bears roamed across the country. Today, only a handful of each remains. The map opposite shows South Korea's main vegetation zones— or what grows where. The only areas of true wilderness left are the mountain forests. Most of the country's 20 national parks protect these highland habitats and animals. Others protect marine and coastal areas.

▶ There are between 7,000 and 9,000 wild Saker falcons in the world. The birds are sometimes illegally caught to use in hunting.

Species at Risk

Nearly all of South Korea's lowland areas have been turned into fields or have been built on. That has taken away the habitat of many of the country's wading birds, such as the impressive hooded crane. The cranes have been coming to South Korea annually for millions of years. Harvested and empty fields now serve as feeding and resting sites for the birds, and the provincial government has proclaimed a crane protection area near West Taegu.

The following are some of South Korea's endangered species:

> Asiatic black bear
> Baikal teal (bird)
> Chinese egret
> Common otter
> Crested ibis (bird)
> Dhole (Asian red dog)
> Gray whale
> Hooded crane
> Japanese night heron

> Musk deer
> Oriental stork
> Purple emperor (butterfly)
> Saker falcon
> Scaly-sided merganser (duck)
> Short-fin mako (shark)
> Siberian tiger
> Steller's sea eagle

NORTH KOREA

Military Demarcation Line,
July 27, 1953

WHITE-NAPED CRANES,
page 21

East Sea
(Sea of Japan)

Seorak
Mountain
N.P.

Taebaek Mountains

Odae
Mountain
N.P.

Bukhan
Mountain N.P.

★ Seoul

Military Demarcation Line,
July 27, 1953

Incheon
(Inch'ŏn)

Han

Chiak
Mountain
N.P.

TIGERS IN
AMUSEMENT PARK,
pages 2, 16-17

Han

Worak
Mountain N.P.

Sobaek
Mountain
N.P.

Taean
Seashore N.P.

Songni
Mountain
N.P.

Sobaek Mountains

Andong
Lake

Geum

Juwang
Mountain N.P.

Yellow
Sea

Daejeon
(Taejŏn)

Deokyu
Mountain
N.P.

Gaya
Mountain
N.P.

Gyeongju
N.P.

Daegu
(Taegu)

Byeonsan
Peninsula N.P.

Naejang
Mountain N.P.

Nakdong

Ulsan

Jiri Mountain
N.P.

Nakdong
River Mouth N.P.

Busan (Pusan)

Gwangju
(Kwangju)

WOODLAND IN FALL,
page 20

Wolchul
Mountain
N.P.

Geoje

Korea Strait

Hallyeo
Marine N.P.

JAPAN

Dadohae
Marine
N.P.

Dadohae
Marine
N.P.

MAP KEY

**Primary Vegetation
Zones/Ecosystems**

Temperate broadleaf forest

**Protected
Lands**

National park

0   miles   50

0   km   50

Jeju
(Cheju I.)

Halla
Mountain N.P.

Vegetation & Ecosystems Map

▲ Students stroll along a tree-lined path on Namhae Island in early fall as the leaves begin to change.

Beneath the Trees

Two-thirds of South Korea is covered by thick forests. Most of it grows on the slopes of the country's rugged mountains. Any areas of lowland forests and the floors of wide valleys were cleared of trees more than a thousand years ago by the first farmers to settle in Korea. However, people also needed to keep warm during South Korea's freezing winters, and so they collected firewood from the mountain forests to heat their homes. As a result, much of the country's forests have been cut down and regrown many times over the centuries.

Forest Life

Most of South Korea's forests are a mixture of deciduous trees, such as Japanese oaks, hornbeams, and Korean maples, and evergreen conifers. Deciduous trees lose their leaves in fall. Conifers grow mainly in colder areas, such as the northern slopes of mountains. They include the Korean big cone pine and Manchurian fir.

The Korean forests also contain many interesting smaller plants. The easiest to see are those that grow on the rocks or cliffs, where trees cannot take root.

▲ **White-naped cranes spend the winter in the DMZ and fly north to breed in Russia and China.**

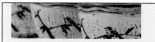

LIVING BETWEEN THE GUNS

One of the few places in Korea where wildlife can exist untouched is the Demilitarized Zone (DMZ). The DMZ is a strip of land 2½ miles (4 km) wide that runs the entire length of the border separating South Korea from North Korea. It was set up in 1953 as part of the ceasefire that ended the Korean War. For over fifty years, hardly anyone has been into it, although about two million soldiers watch each other from either side. One unexpected result is that the DMZ has become a haven for wildlife that lives without being disturbed by humans. Cranes and many other rare Korean birds spend the winter there. If tigers still survive anywhere in Korea—some experts say they do not—they live in the DMZ. If the DMZ ever goes, conservationists are ready to make it a world-renowned nature reserve.

▲ **Barbed wire guards South Korea's highest observation post in the DMZ.**

They include rock jasmines, which produce little white flowers, purple irises, and spiraea shrubs. The most famous South Korean shrub is the Rose of Sharon, which Koreans call *mugunghwa*. *Mugung* means immortality and *hwa* means flower. The bush produces beautiful flowers in a range of pinks, purples, and reds. The mugunghwa is the country's national flower. It is said to symbolize the immortality, determination, and perseverance of the Korean people.

▼ The call of the dhole, or Asiatic wild dog, is like a strange whistle. The dogs use it to call a pack together when animals become separated in dense forest.

Hot and Steamy

On Jeju Island and along a narrow strip in the extreme south of the country, the forests are more like tropical jungles. Here the trees are evergreen—they do not drop their leaves all at once—and they have wide leaves with pointed tips. These "drip tips" help heavy rain flow off the trees. The jungle grows in this region because of the high rainfall and humidity. The southern coast of Jeju Island receives 70 inches (180 cm) of rain a year.

Fly-away Birds

There are no mammals or birds that live only in South Korea and so Korean wildlife is similar to that in China and Siberia. Many of the country's birds, such as the Baikal teal and the swan goose, fly south from Siberia

THE BEAR TRADE

In traditional Korean medicine, the gallbladder of the moon bear has great healing powers. Scientists say there is no evidence that this is true, but some Koreans still eat the organ to treat diabetes, heart disease, and liver problems. People also make stew from the bears' paws. They think the meal will give them extra strength.

As a result almost all of the moon bears in South Korea have been killed. No one is sure how many remain in the wild, but it might be as few as 20. They are protected by law. So Koreans import the gallbladders of moon bears hunted in other parts of Asia. They even use the organs taken from American black bears that have been hunted illegally in Canada. The world's governments are working to stop

▲ The Asiatic black bear has a pale muzzle and a crescent-shaped cream marking on the chest that has led to its popular name of moon bear.

black bears from being hunted. However, a bowl of bear-paw stew sells for $1,000, and a gallbladder is worth ten times that, so people will likely always hunt the bears for profit.

to avoid the bitter cold of the northern winter. In spring they return north to breed. Black-faced spoonbills, on the other hand, spend the summer breeding on the islands around Korea's southern tip. In the winter they fly south to Taiwan and Vietnam.

Although the demand for land and resources has put much of Korea's natural vegetation and wildlife under threat, national parks protect over 6 percent of the land. South Korea's oldest park, Jirisan National Park, is also its largest. Founded in 1967, it is famous in South Korea for its "Ten Sceneries," which include spectacular mountain views, waterfalls, the fall colors of the Piagol Valley, and the Royal Azalea Plateau, which blazes with color in the spring.

At
War
With
Itself

SOUTH KOREAN SOLDIERS keep a permanent watch at the border. They are always ready to fight off an invasion from North Korea. In the minds of some Koreans, they are still at war. The Korean War (1950–53), in which South Korea managed to maintain its existence, has never officially ended. People from the two Koreas cannot travel freely to each other's areas, and many families have been separated. There is one crossing point, at the village of Panmunjeom in the DMZ, but getting permission to move from one side to the other requires a lot of paperwork. The border's fences and barbed wire are a constant reminder of the violence of Korea's past. Even so, many North and South Koreans live in hope that one day Korea will be a single country again.

◀ **UN troops stare across the border at Panmunjeom, the only border crossing point with North Korea.**

ANCIENT KOREANS

People have been living in Korea for at least 10,000 years. The first Koreans hunted animals and gathered plants for food. Many collected shellfish from rivers and along the shore. Stone tools from 3000 B.C. have been found across the peninsula. Archaeologists can see similarities between these objects and ancient stone tools used in Mongolia and Siberia, and so they believe that the ancestors of today's Koreans came from that part of the world.

During the eighth century B.C., people began to make bronze hoes for digging fields and sickles for cutting crops. These farmers dug into hillsides to make hollows in which to build their huts. The hut floors were raised off the ground, which helped keep them dry during the freezing winters.

Each small tribe buried its leaders under stones when they died. Similar tombs were found in China, showing that Korean culture once extended there.

Time line

The chart shows the approximate dates for some of the major ruling dynasties of Korea. Until World War II (1939–1945), Korea was a united nation with no division between North and South.

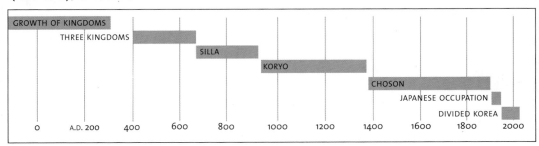

RUSSIA

CHINA

miles 100
0
km 100
0

NORTH
KOREA

East Sea
(Sea of Japan)

Yalu

Yalu

Kangnam Range

Nangnim
Mountains

Hamgyong
Mountains

Korea
Bay

Tongjoson
Bay

Taedong

P'yŏngyang

BORDER CROSSING,
pages 2-3, 24-25

TANKS CROSSING RIVER,
page 33

Baengnyeong

Panmunjeom

Taebaek
Mountains

Ulleung

Songha
Sindang

Incheon
(Inch'ŏn)

Seoul

Han

SOUTH
KOREA

MUSEUM VISIT,
page 33
AND
MEMORIAL DAY,
page 34

Ammyeon

Sobaek
Mountains

BURIAL MOUNDS,
page 28

Yellow
Sea

Daejeon
(Taejŏn)

Nakdong

Daegu
(Taegu)

Ssanggye-sa

Gwangju
(Kwangju)

Busan
(Pusan)

Korea Strait

MAP KEY
Three Kingdoms (A.D. 300–350)

Koguryo

Paekche

Silla

Tombs (before A.D. 935)

Other site

Selected city

Present-day boundaries, drainage,
and place names are shown.

Jeju Strait

Jeju
(Cheju Island)

JAPAN

Historical Map

Tribal Power

Many legends describe Korea's early history. One tells how HwanWoong, the son of heaven, came to Earth and got married. His wife was no ordinary woman; she had been born a bear. She had a son, Tan'gun,

▲ **Mounded tombs dominate the city of Gyeongju, which was once the capital of Silla.**

who became the king of Old Chosun (Joseon). That is where the legend merges with history. Old Chosun was the first kingdom in Korea to learn to use iron. Iron weapons made the Chosun stronger than their neighbors. The Chosun expanded their territory across northwest Korea and into what is now China.

COZY TOES

The Chosun built homes with central heating. The heat was provided by a furnace, which fed hot smoke through passages under the floor. The floor was made of stone slabs, which stayed warm for a long time once heated by the smoke. This heating system is known as an *ondol*, and it is still used in traditional Korean houses today. Ondols warm the sleeping and seating areas. An extra-warm spot is kept reserved for guests.

The Three Kingdoms

Old Chosun ruled for more than 22 centuries, until in 108 B.C. they were overthrown by powerful Chinese armies. For centuries after that, tribes formed alliances that shifted power around the Korean peninsula.

During the first century B.C. and the first century A.D., three new kingdoms emerged: Koguryo, Paekche, and Silla. Koguryo (ko-guh-ryuh) was the largest. It stretched from the Han River in the south into Manchuria in the north.

Most of today's South Korea was split between Silla and Paekche.

A Single Nation

Silla's military strength grew faster than that of its neighbors. In the 660s it made an alliance with the Tang dynasty in China. With the help of Chinese troops, it conquered Paekche and Koguryo. Silla's army then turned on its Chinese allies and forced them out of Korea in 676.

The kings of Silla ruled Korea for more than 200 years, but they began to lose support. The nobles who helped govern the kingdom wanted more power for themselves. By 901 Silla had broken up into three kingdoms again. For ordinary Koreans, it was a time of

▲ The sound made by this ancient bell would have played an important role in Buddhist temple ceremonies.

KINGS OF SILLA

The kingdom of Silla was the first nation to conquer the whole of Korea. At first Silla was run by the Council of Nobles; the king was not all powerful. The elders of each tribe in the kingdom helped make many decisions.

However, once Silla took over the whole of Korea, the noblemen's power was slowly removed by the king. Eventually the country was governed from a central office in the capital of Kumsong (now the town of Gyeongju).

Much of what we know about Silla culture comes from its impressive tombs at Kyongju. For hundred of years Silla's kings and

▲ Archaeologists excavate a Silla tomb— about 200 such tombs have survived.

generals were buried under huge mounds of earth there. You had to be very important to be buried in this way, and to show that the bodies were accompanied by many golden ornaments and other luxuries.

disorder. Many turned to religion. They became Pure Land Buddhists. This branch of Buddhism is still the most popular religion in Korea. Its followers believe they will go to a place of harmony when they die.

From Koryo to Korea

The peninsula was not divided for long. In 936 a powerful noble named Wang Kon unified the Korean kingdoms to create Koryo. Its territory reached north to the Yalu River, which became Korea's border with China. A new government emerged, run by a civil service—a group of people trained to run the country. The civil servants followed the rules of behavior set down by the ancient Chinese teacher Confucius. Confucius taught the value of respect for authority and experience.

In 1392 a family named the Yi seized the throne in Korea. It began a dynasty named the Choson (or Joseon) that ruled until 1910—twenty-six kings in all.

Peaceful Times

Korea entered a long period of peace. The government built better irrigation systems to water the fields, so farmers could grow more rice and other food.

▲ This ceramic monkey and its baby held water for a scholar to use when mixing ink for writing and drawing. It was made in Korea in the 12th century.

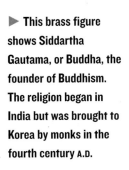

▶ This brass figure shows Siddartha Gautama, or Buddha, the founder of Buddhism. The religion began in India but was brought to Korea by monks in the fourth century A.D.

Farmers did not only grow crops to feed their families. They also grew other crops to sell in markets, such as ginseng, a plant used in traditional medicine. As Koreans earned money from trade, many could afford to educate their children. Art and literature became popular with everyone, not just nobles. A great attraction on market day was the pansori—a musical play performed for the crowds.

Foreigners Visit Korea

In 1656 a Dutch merchant ship ran aground on Jeju. The crew were the first Europeans to reach Korea. They were taken prisoner, but thirteen years later one, Hendrik Hamel, found his way home. His account of his experiences inspired European merchants to set off for Korea to find new trading opportunities. However, European and American ships were banned from visiting Korean ports until the 19th century. Koreans resented the idea of foreigners coming to their country, partly because they tried to convert Koreans to Christianity. In 1864 Korean troops sank the U.S. merchant ship *General Sherman*. They chased away ships from other nations than China.

Korea Gets Closer to Japan

Without foreign trade, Korea soon grew poor, so King Kojong opened his ports again, this time to Japanese ships. China objected, so it

◄ A miniature bronze ten-story pagoda like this would have been offered in a temple as a gift.

▼ This cartoon suggests Japan and a reluctant China were trampling Korea, watched by a nervous Russia. Control of Korea gave Japan a base in mainland Asia from which its neighbors feared it might try to expand its power even farther.

was given trading rights, too. Soon the United States and others were trading with Korea again.

Korea began to modernize quickly. It bought new equipment to build factories, mainly from Japan. But the government spent more than it could afford, and raised taxes to pay its debts. The workers revolted in 1894 and almost managed to take over the country. The Chinese sent soldiers to support the government, and so did the Japanese.

Soon the two foreign armies were fighting for control of Korea. They were joined by Russia. The Japanese defeated the Chinese and Russians and made Korea a colony. In 1910 Japan was given legal control of Korea by an international treaty. The Japanese set up a ruthless and cruel military government. On March 1, 1919, two million angry Koreans demonstrated in Seoul and most other provinces against the presence of the Japanese in their country. The Japanese army broke up the protest and killed 7,500 people.

Split in Two

In 1941 Japan entered World War II (1939–1945) against the United States and its allies. It was defeated and surrendered in August 1945. The victors in the

war, including Britain, the Soviet Union, and the United States, took charge of Japan's old territory, including Korea. They agreed that Soviet troops should occupy the northern half of Korea while U.S. troops stayed in the southern part. They aimed eventually to be able to rebuild a unified Korea. But the Americans were

▲ South Korean tanks on a training exercise cross the river near Seoul.

▼ A U.S. military airplane on display in a museum reminds visitors of the Korean War.

THE KOREAN WAR

In 1948 Korea had two official governments. The elected government in Seoul was supported by the West. The communist ruler of the north, Kim Il Sung, was supported by the Soviet Union. Both governments claimed to rule the whole of Korea.

On June 25, 1950, Kim Il Sung invaded the south. His troops were armed with Soviet tanks. South Korea was defended mainly by policemen with pistols.

On June 27 the United Nations (UN) asked foreign nations to fight with the South Koreans. The U.S. forces were the first in, but they could not halt the communists' advance. By August the UN forces were pushed into a pocket around the port of Busan. But the UN forces soon hit back, landing troops at Incheon and Wonsan. The North Korean army collapsed under these attacks. Now it was their turn to retreat. The South Korean and UN forces chased them north. By November 1950 some southern units had even reached the Chinese border at the Yalu River. It looked like the war would soon be over.

Then the tables turned yet again. China, which the year before had become a communist country, adopting a political system similar to that of the Soviet Union, joined forces with the North Koreans. Nearly half a million communist troops fought their way back south. By January 1951 two huge armies faced each across a front line that divided the country close to the original border between north and south.

Fighting continued for the next two years, but both sides knew they could not win. They began to negotiate for peace. The guns stopped finally on July 27, 1953. Neither side gave up its claim to the other's territory, and the two armies were separated by a strip of no-man's-land that followed the border: the Demilitarized Zone. The U.S. Army is still there. More than 50 years after the end of the war, 37,000 U.S. troops still assist South Koreans in defending the border. Some South Koreans, however, are beginning to call for the troops to leave.

◀ **Kindergarten children in Seoul pray at the graves of people who died in the Korean War as part of the annual memorial day ceremonies.**

LONG TIME NO SEE!

A divided Korea has meant that some families were cut in two. Members of these families have had little or no contact with their relatives for more than 50 years. Many of the South Koreans awaiting news from the north are the relatives of prisoners who never came home after the war.

In 2000 the two governments agreed to allow family reunions, giving many elderly Koreans a chance to finally see their relatives. In 2002 the governments agreed to build a permanent site for reunions in the North Korean mountain resort of Kumgang. However, in 2006 relations soured. The reunions have now been stopped, and the Kumgang center is unlikely to be built.

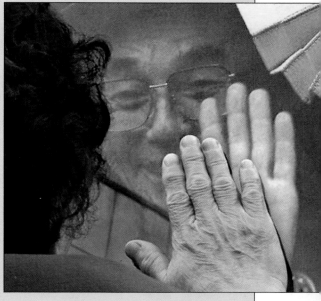

▲ **A North Korean says goodbye to his South Korean daughter through a bus window after a family reunion in 2000.**

suspicious of the Soviets and of communism, the Soviet Union's political system. Korea became a front line in the Cold War, a stand-off between the communist nations and the democracies in the West.

War and Peace

The Soviets set up a communist government in the north, and the south set up its own pro-American administration. U.S. troops left southern Korea in 1949. In 1950 the communists invaded. The result was the Korean War, which raged until 1953. More than 2.5 million people—Koreans, U.S., Chinese, and other foreign soldiers—died. Korea remained divided: But now the two Koreas were sworn enemies and have stayed so ever since.

Festivals and *Formality*

IN MAY, ALL OF SOUTH KOREA throws a party to celebrate the birthday of Buddha, the prince who founded the Buddhist religion over 2,500 years ago. From the time of the Three Kingdoms, Koreans have celebrated Buddha's birthday by decorating their homes and streets with colorful paper lanterns. Many families write a prayer on a piece of paper and slip it into a lantern to bring good luck.

Today Buddha's Birthday is a national holiday, and everyone joins in street parties and dances. The highlight of the holiday is the Lotus Lantern Parade in the capital, Seoul, when huge lanterns are carried through the city. Buddhists travel from across the world to take part in the parade, which ends at the city's Jogyesa Temple.

◀ **Thousands of Buddhists carry paper lamps through Seoul as part of the 2005 celebrations of Buddha's Birthday.**

A GROWING POPULATION

The population of South Korea has more than doubled in the last 50 years to nearly 50 million people. That is in spite of the fact that many South Koreans have left the country. Nearly two million moved to live in the United States, for example. Meanwhile, more than four million refugees moved from North to South Korea when Korea was split in the 1950s.

In the past South Korean families were very large, but today the government encourages people to have smaller families. Most people now have just one or two children.

▶ **South Korea's cities are some of the most densely populated places in the world.**

Common Korean Phrases

Here are a few words and phrases you might use in South Korea. There are no stresses on different parts of words as you pronounce them. Give them a try:

Yeoboseyo? (Yaw boh seh yoh?)
  Hello (answering telephone)
Annyeonghaseyo (Ahn yawng hah seh yoh?)
  How are you?
Annyeonghi kaseyo (Ahn yawng hee kah seh yoh)
  Goodbye (to someone leaving)
Annyeonghi kyeseyo (Ahn yawng hee kyeh seh yoh)
  Goodbye (when you are leaving)
Kamsahamnida (Kam sa ham nee da) Thank you
Cheonmaneyo (Chawn mahn neh yoh)
  You're welcome
Ne (Neh)   Yes
Aniyo (Ah nee yoh)   No
Yeong-eo hashimnikka? (Yawng-aw hash eem nee ka?)
  Do you speak English?

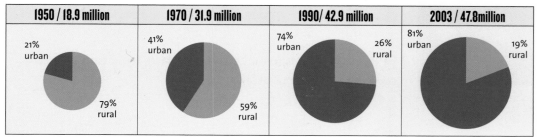

1950 / 18.9 million	1970 / 31.9 million	1990 / 42.9 million	2003 / 47.8 million
21% urban / 79% rural	41% urban / 59% rural	74% urban / 26% rural	81% urban / 19% rural

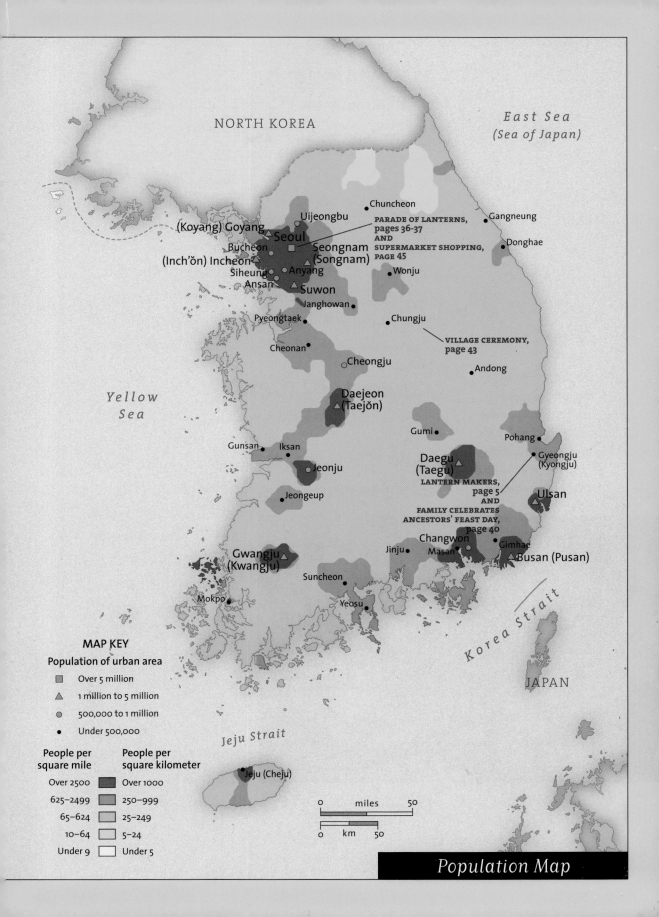

NORTH KOREA

*East Sea
(Sea of Japan)*

Chuncheon

PARADE OF LANTERNS,
pages 36-37
AND
SUPERMARKET SHOPPING,
PAGE 45

Gangneung

Donghae

Uijeongbu

(Koyang) Goyang

Seoul

Bucheon

Seongnam
(Songnam)

(Inch'ŏn) Incheon

Siheung

Anyang

Ansan

Suwon

Wonju

Janghowan

Pyeongtaek

Cheonan

Chungju

Cheongju

VILLAGE CEREMONY,
page 43

Andong

*Yellow
Sea*

Daejeon
(Taejŏn)

Gumi

Pohang

Gunsan

Iksan

Daegu
(Taegu)

Gyeongju
(Kyongju)

Jeonju

LANTERN MAKERS,
page 5
AND
FAMILY CELEBRATES
ANCESTORS' FEAST DAY,
page 40

Ulsan

Jeongeup

Changwon

Gwangju
(Kwangju)

Jinju

Masan

Gimhae

Busan (Pusan)

Suncheon

Mokpo

Yeosu

Korea Strait

JAPAN

MAP KEY

Population of urban area

▪ Over 5 million

▲ 1 million to 5 million

● 500,000 to 1 million

• Under 500,000

Jeju Strait

Jeju (Cheju)

People per square mile	People per square kilometer
Over 2500	Over 1000
625–2499	250–999
65–624	25–249
10–64	5–24
Under 9	Under 5

0   miles   50

0   km   50

Population Map

Getting Along

Compared with many countries, South Korea often seems quiet and reserved. People are polite and formal. They follow rules to avoid having arguments in public or causing embarrassment to other people. These rules are based on Confucianism. They influence every part of life in South Korea. They organize relationships between people into types. Each requires a certain way of behaving. The five relationships are those between employer and employee, parent and child, husband and wife, young person and old person, and between friends.

Respect for Elders

Children learn from an early age to do as they are told by their parents. That does not change, even when the children grow up. Adults must also respect their parents or other older relatives. At the beginning of the year, everyone travels to their family home to celebrate Sol, the Korean New Year. The family puts on traditional clothes. The younger family members bow to their parents and grandparents and promise to respect and obey them throughout the year.

▼ Members of one of South Korea's noble families celebrate their ancestors' feast day. The formal ceremony follows strict rules originally laid down by Confucianism.

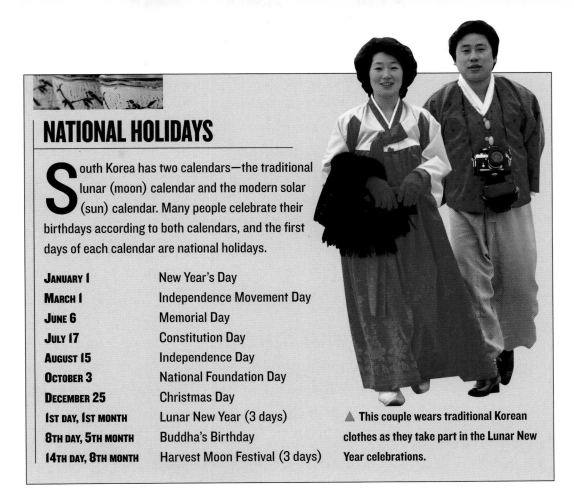

NATIONAL HOLIDAYS

South Korea has two calendars—the traditional lunar (moon) calendar and the modern solar (sun) calendar. Many people celebrate their birthdays according to both calendars, and the first days of each calendar are national holidays.

JANUARY 1	New Year's Day
MARCH 1	Independence Movement Day
JUNE 6	Memorial Day
JULY 17	Constitution Day
AUGUST 15	Independence Day
OCTOBER 3	National Foundation Day
DECEMBER 25	Christmas Day
1ST DAY, 1ST MONTH	Lunar New Year (3 days)
8TH DAY, 5TH MONTH	Buddha's Birthday
14TH DAY, 8TH MONTH	Harvest Moon Festival (3 days)

▲ This couple wears traditional Korean clothes as they take part in the Lunar New Year celebrations.

The family then pays its respects to its dead ancestors. Only men can perform the rituals. Families who only have daughters are thought not to please their ancestors, so many parents prefer to have sons. In the past, some very poor families even left baby girls to die because they did not want them. This does not happen today, and the numbers of male and female South Koreans are quite balanced.

Lightening Up
Although everyday life may seem very formal, South Koreans have a lot of fun. After the New Year

ceremonies, families traditionally visit the homes of their neighbors to say "Happy New Year." A long party starts—but it does not stay in one place. Everyone dances and sings as they move from house to house around the neighborhood. The biggest parties are held during Chusok, the Harvest Moon Festival. Like many South Korean holidays, the exact date of the celebration depends on the position of the moon. Families thank their ancestors for providing them with rice and fruits.

Gods and Spirits

Korean Buddhists try to lead a pure life so they can become enlightened, or filled with wisdom. Buddhists believe that when an enlightened person dies, he or

WORSHIPING THE SPIRITS

According to legend, every village in Korea has a *sonang*, or mountain spirit. Rivers and lakes are ruled by dragons. The head of each village performs rituals at a shrine to please the local spirits, and also asks them for signs to predict the future. One ritual involves burning rice paper. If the ashes rise above the flames, the village will have a good year. When the ashes settle to the ground, the village has trouble ahead. If evil spirits are causing problems, female priests called *mudang* are called in to remove them. While the mudang is at work, all the villagers must stay indoors, so they do not make the shrine unclean. Although fewer people believe in sonang, today 40,000 mudang still work in South Korea.

▲ Families gather at tombs to offer food to the spirits of their ancestors.

she is freed from all suffering. A person attains a blissful state called nirvana.

Christianity was brought to Korea by European priests in the 17th century. In the past it was often attacked as being un-Korean, because it came from another culture. Today, however, about a third of South Koreans are Christian.

All South Koreans, even Buddhists and Christians, are influenced by Confucian rules in how they live. But another strong influence binds South Korean society:

▲ Villagers perform an ancient ceremony called *Chishingbalgi*, or Trampling the Devils, to drive demons out of their village.

the spirits. Ancient Koreans worshipped the spirits of their ancestors as well as spirits that inhabit natural features, such as mountains. Some modern Koreans also often perform rituals relating to the spirits.

Making a Match

In the past, all marriages in Korea were arranged by the families of the bride and groom. These arranged marriages are still common, although the young men and women are rarely forced to marry each other

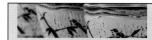

HAPPY BIRTHDAY BABY!

In the past newborn babies in South Korea often died after just a few weeks. Today, although a baby's chances of a long life are among the highest in the world, parents still celebrate the growth of their babies in the traditional way. When a baby is 100 days old, the family holds a feast. The spirits of the family's grandmothers are given rice and soup to thank them for watching over the baby, while the family eats sweet rice and bean cakes.

An even larger celebration takes place on the child's first birthday. Again the spirits join the feast, but this time the child also forecasts his or her future. The child is seated at a table displaying several objects. The object he or she picks up first shows what the future holds. A pen or a book means the child will be a scholar. Future business people grab money or rice, while a child who chooses a cake will work for the government. The choice of a thread means a long life.

if they do not get along. Today, young South Koreans also get married after simply meeting and falling in love with a partner.

Before a wedding goes ahead, the bride and groom consult a fortune-teller. The fortune-teller uses the couple's exact dates and times of birth to check whether they will be happy together. If their fortune looks unlucky, the wedding might even be canceled!

Korean weddings have many traditions, but not many couples have a completely old-fashioned

▲ A bride rides in a cart pulled by members of the wedding party in this traditional wedding celebration.

CRAM IT IN

South Koreans go to school from age six to age eighteen. The school system is similar to that of the United States, with six grades of elementary school, three grades of middle school, and then another three of high school. After graduating high school, most students are expected to go to college, but the competition for places is great. Colleges have an extremely tough entrance exam so they can select the best students. To make sure that their children are successful in the exams, wealthy parents send them to extra classes at *hagwons*, or cram schools. Hagwons teach children in the evening and give so much homework that students often work until well after midnight and then begin to study again at 6 A.M.

◀ Girls study in a crowded classroom. Teaching is quite old-fashioned: Students who fail exams are punished with extra homework.

ceremony. The bride might wear a white gown instead of the *hanbok*, the traditional Korean dress. The groom dresses in a suit, instead of loose pants and a long coat. Weddings often take place in a rented hall; previously, they were always held at the bride's house. However, the couple still share traditional foods and bow formally to guests and family members.

It is also traditional for families to give newlyweds a pair of wooden ducks. The groom's mother may throw a duck to the bride to catch in her dress. It is believed that if she catches it, her first baby will be a boy. If she drops the duck, she will have a daughter.

▲ A young boy tastes a strip of kimchi—pickled vegetable—in a supermarket in Seoul. There are many different varieties to try.

Eating Korean Style

More tradition surrounds Korean food. One popular dish is *kimchi*, which is a mixture of pickled vegetables. This used to be eaten throughout the winter, when no fresh vegetables were available, because pickling vegetables stops them from going bad and helps them to last longer. Cooks still make a lot of kimchi in November, as winter approaches. Perhaps the most familiar Korean dish is *bulgoki*, also known as Korean barbecue, strips of spicy meat grilled on a hotplate at the table.

South Korean families eat together, sitting on the floor around the table. Each person has a bowl of rice or soup. The diners share the other dishes—usually fish, beef, tofu (bean curd), or kimchi. They pick up food with chopsticks. Ginseng, ginger, and green teas are popular hot drinks.

▼ Drums are everywhere in Korea. This temple drum was beaten to call monks to prayer.

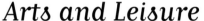

Arts and Leisure

Korean music is played on a number of instruments that look odd to Westerners. They include the *heagum*, a violin with only two strings. Perhaps the most unusual Korean art form is puppeteering. The performer hangs a puppet on his or her foot, which is pushed through a curtain in front of the audience. The puppeteer uses his hands to control long rods that move the puppet's arms and legs.

South Korea also has many types of traditional dance. Some dances are very lively, such as the whirling drum dance. Other dances are much slower and involve precise movements. They were first performed for the royal family. These formal dances were made popular around the world by Choe Sung-Hee, Korea's greatest dancer. She became known as the Flower of Korea and toured the world in the 1930s and 1940s.

The most popular sport in South Korea is soccer (called football in Korea). The country co-hosted the World Cup finals with Japan in 2002. Football fever swept the nation as the South Korean team, called the "Red Devils," reached the semifinals.

Taekwondo—"the art of hand and foot fighting"—is the most popular martial art in Korea. It was developed from the ancient martial arts which helped train Korean nobles to become skilled warriors.

▼ **South Korean fans celebrate the country's first-ever victory in the World Cup finals. Their team beat Poland 2–0 in the 2002 tournament, which South Korea co-hosted.**

The Tiger Roars

N SEPTEMBER 1988 the world's eyes were on Seoul as the Olympic flame was lit at the start of the 24th Summer Olympic Games. South Koreans saw it as the moment when their country finally became a modern democracy and economic power. They were pleased to put an end to years of war, corruption, and scandal. The Olympic flame was carried into the stadium by 76-year-old Sohn Kee-chung. He had become a national hero for South Koreans by winning an Olympic gold medal in 1936, when he set a world record for the marathon. In 1948 he carried the South Korean flag at the opening of the London Olympics, the first games attended by Korea after the end of the Second World War, when the country was divided.

◄ The 1988 Olympic flame is lit by the final torch bearers—students who represented sports, the sciences, and the arts.

POWER AND THE PEOPLE

The official name of South Korea is the Republic of Korea (ROK). That is because its government claims to be in charge of the whole of Korea and does not recognize North Korea as a separate country. In reality, the region is still divided, and the ROK government controls only South Korea. This area is divided into nine *do*, or provinces. The largest cities: Busan, Daegu, Incheon, Gwangju, and Daejeon are governed separately by an elected council. The capital, Seoul, has a special status as the seat of the national government. Each province has an elected governor, and most cities also have a mayor. Provinces are further divided into *gun*, or counties.

▶ **Korean protestors near a U.S. Army base hold signs saying that the foreign troops should leave Korea.**

Trading Partners

South Korea has one of the strongest economies in Eastern Asia, an area of the world where business has been booming over the last 20 years. Most of South Korea's wealth comes from manufacturing and service industries, such as banking. It exports ships, cars, computers, and other electronic items. It imports the raw materials to make those products, as well as all the oil needed by the country. South Korea's main trading partners are its close neighbors Japan and China.

Country	Percent Korea exports
China	27.3%
United States	14.6%
Japan	8.5%
All others combined	49.6%

Country	Percent Korea imports
Japan	18.5%
China	14.8%
United States	11.8%
Saudi Arabia	6.2%
All others combined	48.7%

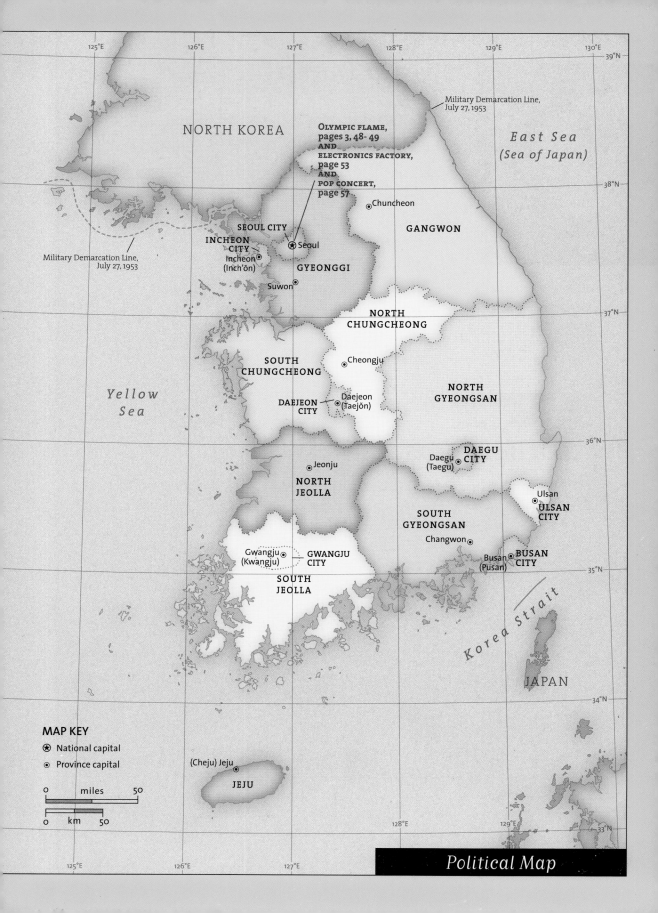

NORTH KOREA

East Sea
(Sea of Japan)

Military Demarcation Line,
July 27, 1953

**OLYMPIC FLAME,
pages 3, 48- 49
AND
ELECTRONICS FACTORY,
page 53
AND
POP CONCERT,
page 57**

⊙ Chuncheon

GANGWON

SEOUL CITY
**INCHEON
CITY**
Incheon
(Inch'ŏn) ⊙
⊛ Seoul

GYEONGGI

⊙ Suwon

Military Demarcation Line,
July 27, 1953

**NORTH
CHUNGCHEONG**

*Yellow
Sea*

**SOUTH
CHUNGCHEONG**

⊙ Cheongju

**NORTH
GYEONGSAN**

**DAEJEON
CITY**
Daejeon ⊙
(Taejŏn)

**DAEGU
CITY**
Daegu ⊙
(Taegu)

⊙ Jeonju

**NORTH
JEOLLA**

Ulsan
⊛ **ULSAN
CITY**

**SOUTH
GYEONGSAN**

Changwon ⊙

Gwangju ⊙
(Kwangju)
**GWANGJU
CITY**

Busan ⊛ **BUSAN
CITY**
(Pusan)

**SOUTH
JEOLLA**

Korea Strait

JAPAN

MAP KEY

⊛ National capital

⊙ Province capital

0   miles   50

0   km   50

(Cheju) Jeju ⊙
JEJU

Political Map

Tiger in Turmoil

When fighting between North and South Korea stopped in 1953, the people of South Korea set about rebuilding their country. They were very successful. Today South Korea is one of the East Asian Tigers, along with Singapore, Hong Kong, and Taiwan. The Tigers got their name because of their huge economic growth in the late 20th century. South Korea is the most successful of the Tigers, being the 11th-largest economy in the world—and it is rising fast. The country's recent history has been far from smooth, however. Life has often been hard for ordinary South Koreans.

▲ **A watch celebrates the meeting of South and North Korean leaders in 2000.**

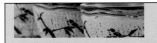

HOW THE GOVERNMENT WORKS

The president is the head of the country and is in charge of the government and the armed forces. He is elected by the people every five years. The president appoints the prime minister and the State Council, which is made up of the ministers in charge of each section of government. Laws are made by the Kuk Hoe (National Assembly). Its 299 members are elected every four years. There are two main political parties. The assembly elections are structured so that each party gets a fair share of seats according to the views of the people. The Supreme Court is in charge of interpreting the laws made by the government. The court's chief judge is appointed jointly by the president and the National Assembly.

SIXTH REPUBLIC		
EXECUTIVE	LEGISLATIVE	JUDICIARY
PRESIDENT	PRIME MINISTER	SUPREME COURT
STATE COUNCIL	NATIONAL ASSEMBLY 299 MEMBERS	DISTRICT COURTS

Toppling Governments

South Korea's first president, Syngman Rhee, led the nation through the Korean War. Rhee had absolute authority. He did not allow any opposition to his policies. He changed the law that stopped him from running for president more than twice and was elected a total of four times. By 1960, his fourth election victory, many people were unhappy that he had governed for so long. Violent protests erupted across the country, and many people died. Rhee resigned and fled to Hawaii.

A new government took over. It was led by a prime minister instead of a president and run by a cabinet of ministers. However, the government was removed from power by an army general, Park Chung Hee, a year later. Park banned political activity and

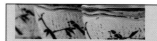

MIRACLE ON THE HAN

In the 1950s South Korea produced little more than rice. It needed aid money from abroad to keep going. In the 1960s the government began a program of economic development. Certain companies were helped to expand very quickly, while the government made sure that their workers did not earn much money. As a result South Korea could make products very cheaply and sell them around the world. Within 30 years the country was a leading manufacturer of cars, ships, chemicals, and high-tech products, such as computers.

In 1962 a typical South Korean earned $87 a year. By 1989 the average income had shot up to nearly $5,000. Economists called the boom the "Miracle on the Han" (after the river in Seoul) because South Korea's growth was similar to West Germany's "Miracle on the Rhine" after World War II ended in 1945. The miracle brought change. For centuries rich landowners had ruled over ordinary people. Today a large middle class is wealthy enough to control their own lives.

▼ A woman produces electronic parts for watches and televisions in a Seoul factory.

INDUSTRIAL CENTERS AND PORTS

The map shows the location of South Korea's industrial centers. The country has almost no natural resources of its own. Nearly all of the raw materials it needs—gas, iron, and oil—are imported. As a result it has several large ports, including Busan, Incheon (for Seoul), Ulsan, and Jeju. The main centers of manufacturing are close to these ports. Seoul is also a regional center for banking and financial services.

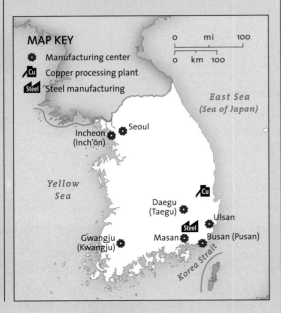

MAP KEY
- Manufacturing center
- Cu Copper processing plant
- Steel Steel manufacturing

0   mi   100
0   km   100

East Sea
(Sea of Japan)

Incheon
(Inch'ŏn)   Seoul

Yellow
Sea

Daegu
(Taegu)

Cu

Ulsan

Gwangju
(Kwangju)   Masan   Steel   Busan (Pusan)

Korea Strait

used the army to run the country. In 1963 Park was forced by the United States to restore democracy. The general ran for president himself and won.

Making the Miracle

Park was a very authoritarian leader. If people protested against his government, he sent soldiers to scare them. Demonstrators even got killed. Park did not allow other political parties to operate freely. The press could not report things without government permission. But it was thanks to Park that South Korea grew into one of the richest countries in the world. He began a policy of economic development that changed South Korea from a nation of farmers into a leading manufacturing country.

Political Fixes

Park was elected again in 1967, but his opponents claimed he had fixed the election. When he narrowly won again in 1971, Park decided not to have an elected government any more. He changed the law so that he could be president for as long as he wanted. By 1979 Park had become very unpopular. Riots and demonstrations broke out across the country.

In October, Park was killed by the chief of the secret police, who had been one of his closest friends. The country then fell into the hands of General Chun Doo Hwan, who took over the presidency in 1980. Chun's rule was rocked in 1983 when several members of his government were killed by a bomb in Rangoon, Myanmar. The bomb was planted by North Koreans.

By 1987 Chun was hated by Koreans. He chose Roh Tae Woo as the ruling political party's candidate in the election that year. When Roh became president in 1988, it was the first time in modern South Korean history that power had changed hands without violence.

Business Corruption

The economic boom came about because the government gave its support to the country's largest companies. That helped the companies grow into giant firms, known as *chaebols*. Chaebols expanded very quickly by taking over other firms. They moved into many areas of business, instead of concentrating on one thing. The relationships between the government and chaebols were close—sometimes

▼ One of the most successful South Korean firms was the carmaker Daewoo. It was bought by General Motors in 2001 after a financial crisis had damaged its business.

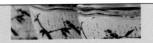

KIM PRIZES PEACE

One man did more than any other to fight for the return of democracy in South Korea. Kim Dae Jung, the son of a farmer, led the opposition to General Park in the 1960s. That was a dangerous job, and Kim was imprisoned twice by the secret police. In 1980 President Chun Doo Hwan sentenced Kim to death but later decided to imprison him for life. In 1982 Kim was allowed to go to the United States for medical treatment. He returned to his country in 1985, and was imprisoned in his home, but ran for president twice before finally winning in 1997.

Kim was 72 when he became leader, but his best work was still to come. He started the Sunshine Policy to improve relations with North Korea. In 2000 Kim became the first South Korean president to meet with the leader of North Korea. They organized reunions of families divided by the frontier. In that year Kim won the Nobel Peace Prize for his work.

▼ A monk reads about the historic meeting between the leaders of North and South Korea.

a little too close. Companies gave money to politicians to make sure that the government continued to support them. It took many years of investigation to clean up South Korea's corrupt business practices. Today the South Korean government is much less closely linked to the chaebols. Many of them are now international corporations known across the world. They include LG, Daewoo, Hyundai, and Samsung.

Modern Times

Since 1988 South Korea has been a peaceful place. The country has even made friends with Russia and China and many other countries that once supported North Korea. Nearly four million tourists visit South Korea each year. Most come from East Asia, but thanks to the Olympic Games and the World Cup, visitors also arrive from farther away.

In 1993 Kim Young Sam became president. He set up investigations into corruption in politics. The investigations even led to the arrest of his own son, along with the ex-presidents Chun and Roh. Kim Dae

THE KOREANS ARE COMING

In the 1960s teenagers in the United States were enjoying the "British Invasion," as new and exciting British pop groups, such as the Rolling Stones and the Beatles, swept the nation. A similar thing is happening today in East Asia with the "Korean Wave."

After centuries of being in the shadow of its two powerful neighbors, Japan and China, South Korea is now the trendiest place in Asia. Stars of Korean pop music, or K-pop, include the boy band Shinhwa—"Legend" in Korean—and the solo stars Kangta and Bada. On television, Korean romantic drama series such as *Winter Sonata* and *Endless Love* are shown to hundreds of millions of viewers across East Asia and beyond, including the United States.

▲ Award-winning group Shinhwa performs at the 2004 MTV Buzz Asia Concert held in Seoul, where they represented South Korea.

Jung was president from 1997 to 2003, when he was succeeded by Roh Moo Hyun.

Today's South Korea has a properly working democracy. Its biggest problem, once again, is its neighbor. After a few years of improving relations, North Korea built a nuclear bomb in 2006. Having such powerful weapons nearby made South Koreans very worried. They are working with international governments to try to resolve this issue peacefully.

▼ Tourists examine giant models of the North and South Korean leaders made to celebrate their meeting in 2000.

Add a Little Extra to Your Country Report!

If you are assigned to write a report about South Korea, you'll want to include basic information about the country, of course. The Fast Facts chart on page 8 will give you a good start. The rest of the book will give you the details you need to create a full and up-to-date paper or PowerPoint presentation. But what can you do to make your report more fun than anyone else's? If you use your imagination and dig a bit deeper into some of the topics introduced in this book, you're sure to come up with information that will make your report unique!

>Flag

Perhaps you could explain the history of South Korea's flag, and the meanings of its colors and symbols. Go to **www.crwflags.com/fotw/flags** for more information.

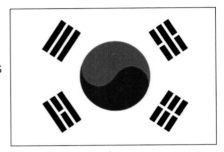

>National Anthem

How about downloading South Korea's national anthem and playing it for your class? At **www.nationalanthems.info** you'll find what you need, including the words to the anthem, plus sheet music for the anthem. Simply pick "K" and then "Korea" from the list on the left-hand side of the screen, and you're on your way.

>Time Difference

If you want to understand the time difference between South Korea and where you are, this Web site can help: **www.worldtimeserver.com**. Just pick "Korea, Republic of" from the list on the left. If you called South Korea right now, would you wake whomever you are calling from their sleep?

>Currency

Another Web site will convert your money into won, the currency used in South Korea. You'll want to know how much money to bring if you're ever lucky enough to travel to South Korea: **www.xe.com/ucc**.

>Weather

Why not check the current weather in South Korea? It's easy—simply go to **www.weather.com** to find out if it's sunny or cloudy, warm or cold in South Korea right this minute! Pick "World" from the headings at the top of the page. Then search for South Korea. Click on any city you like. Be sure to click on the tabs below the weather report for Sunrise/Sunset information, Weather Watch, and Business Travel Outlook, too. Scroll down the page for the 36-hour Forecast and a satellite weather map. Compare your weather to the weather in the South Korean city you chose. Is this a good season, weather-wise, for a person to travel to South Korea?

>Miscellaneous

Still want more information? Simply go to National Geographic's One-Stop Research site at **http://www.nationalgeographic.com/onestop**. It will help you find maps, photos and art, articles and information, games and features that you can use to jazz up your report.

Glossary

Archaeologist a person who studies the remains of ancient people to learn more about how people lived in the past.

Buddhist a person who follows the teachings of Buddhism.

Climate the average weather of a certain place at different times of year.

Communism a system of government where a single political party rules a country with the job of ensuring that wealth is shared equally among all the people in the country. In 1949 Korea was split into two countries: North Korea is communist, while South Korea is a democracy, where people elect leaders to govern them.

Conifer a tree that produces cones instead of flowers. Many conifers also have needles instead of leaves.

Culture a collection of beliefs, traditions, and styles that belongs to people living in a certain part of the world.

Demilitarized where all weapons and troops have been removed.

Dictator a leader who has complete control over a country and does not have to be elected or re-elected to office regularly.

Divine godly; produced by a god.

Economy the system by which a country creates wealth through making and trading in products.

Ecosystem a community of living things and the environment they interact with; an ecosystem includes plants, animals, soil, water, and air.

Endangered an animal or plant that is at risk of dying out.

Gallbladder a small organ near an animal's liver that produces bile, a liquid used to digest food.

Generation the members of a family that are all about the same age—brothers and sisters and their cousins. Their parents are an older generation, while their children are the younger generation.

Guardian a person or body of people who is responsible for the welfare of another person, normally a child.

Habitat a part of the environment that is suitable for certain plants and animals.

Humidity moisture, or water vapor, in the air.

Irrigation taking water from a river or a well to use on fields and in plantations.

Peninsula a narrow piece of land that is surrounded by water on three sides. The word means "almost island" in Latin.

Petroleum oil and gas that is pumped up from beneath the surface of the Earth. Petroleum is refined to make gasoline and other fuels and provides the raw materials for plastics.

Species a type of organism; animals or plants in the same species look similar and can only breed successfully among themselves.

Treaty an agreement between two or more countries.

United Nations (UN) an international organization that includes most of the countries of the world. The UN is where the world's governments discuss the world's problems and figure out how to work together to solve them.

Bibliography

Collinwood, Dean Walter. *Korea: The High and Beautiful Peninsula*. Tarrytown, NY: Benchmark Books, 1997.

De Capua, Sarah. *Korea*. New York, NY: Marshall Cavendish, 2005.

Stickler, John. *Land of Morning Calm: Korean Culture Then and Now*. Fremont, CA: Shen's Books, 2003.

http://www.asianinfo.org/ asianinfo/korea/history.htm (historical information)

http://www.korea.net/korea/ korea.asp (general information)

Further Information

NATIONAL GEOGRAPHIC Articles

Kim, Whanyung. "No Longer the Hermit Kingdom." NATIONAL GEOGRAPHIC TRAVELER (March 2004): 36.

Pang, Deb. "E-Mail from Seoul, S. Korea." NATIONAL GEOGRAPHIC TRAVELER (January/February 2003): 92.

Web sites to explore

More fast facts about South Korea, from the CIA (Central Intelligence Agency): https:// www.cia.gov/cia/publications/ factbook/geos/ ks.html

Would you like to find out more about the role of U.S. and other U.N. forces during the Korean War? Look as this commemorative site by the U.S. Department of Defense: http://korea50.army.mil/ history/index.shtml

What is all the fuss about Korean pop music? Hear the songs for yourself on the K-pop Web site: http://www.kpopmusic.com/ kpop/news.php

Have you ever wanted to make octopus casserole or learn how to make kimchi—Korean pickled vegetables? Look at the Korean recipes and much more on this site: http://www. koreainfogate.com/taste/food/ recipemain.asp

Find out more about Seoul's Lotus Lantern Festival and other aspects of Korean Buddhism by searching through: http://www.korean buddhism.net/

See, hear

There are many ways to get

a taste of life in South Korea, such as movies, music CDs,

magazines, or TV shows. You might be able to locate these:

Sun & Moon: Fairy Tales from Korea
This collection of traditional stories has been translated into English and is highly illustrated to give you a better idea about the customs and culture of South Korea.

Korean Herald
This South Korean newspaper is the main one to be published in English. The newspaper's Web site is the best place to find out about the latest developments in South Korea: http://www.korea herald.co.kr/

Arahan (2004)
A fun action film set in Seoul in which a traffic cop learns an ancient martial art called the "Palm Blast" and is drawn into an action-packed battle between good and evil.

Index

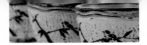

Credits

Picture Credits

Front Cover – Spine: Sz Akos/Shutterstock; Top: H. Edward Kim/NGIC; Low Far Left: Paul Chesley/NGIC; Low Left: Martin Gray/NGIC; Low Right: Michael S. Yamashita/NGIC; Low Far Right: H, Edward Kim/NGIC.

Interior - Alamy: Imagebroker: 18 lo; Motoring Picture Library: 55 lo; Neil Setchfield: 46 lo; Corbis: Ricardo Azoury: 38 lo; David Ball: 11 lo; Bohemian Nomad Picturemakers: 44 up; Jerry Cooke: 3 right, 48–49; Wolfgang Kaehler: 59 up; Catherine Karnow: 2 left, 6–7,12 up; Kim Kyung-Hoon/Reuters: 3 left, 14 up, 36-37, 57 up; Reuters: 34 right, 35 up, 45 lo, 47 lo, 50 lo, 56 lo, 57 lo; Rykoff Collection: 32 lo; Michael Setboun: 44 lo; Seoul Shinmun/epa: TP; John Van Hasselt: 33 lo; NGIC: H Edward Kim: 5 up, 10 up, 11 up, 13 up, 15 lo, 20 up, 26 center, 28 up, 29 up, 29 lo, 30 up, 30 lo, 31 right, 40 up, 41 up, 42 lo, 43 lo, 52 up, 53 lo; Frans Lanting: 22 center; O. Louis Mazzatenta: 23 up; Michael Nichols: 2 right, 16–17; Michael S. Yamashita: 2-3, 21 up, 21 lo, 24–25, 33 up.

Text copyright © 2007 National Geographic Society
Published by the National Geographic Society.
All rights reserved. Reproduction of the whole or any part of the contents without written permission from the National Geographic Society is strictly prohibited. For information about special discounts for bulk purchases, contact National Geographic Special Sales: ngspecsales@ngs.org

For more information, please call 1-800-NGS-LINE (647-5463) or write to the following address:

NATIONAL GEOGRAPHIC SOCIETY
1145 17th Street N.W.
Washington, D.C. 20036-4688 U.S.A.

Visit the Society's Web site at www.nationalgeographic.com

Library of Congress Cataloging-in-Publication Data available on request
ISBN: 978-1-4263-0125-4

Printed in the United States of America

Series design by Jim Hiscott.
The body text is set in Avenir; Knockout.
The display text is set in Matrix Script.

Front Cover—Top: Traffic passes the medieval South Gate in Seoul; Low Far Left: A tiger peers at tourists on a bus; Low Left: Statues of Buddha in the cave temple of Sanbangsa; Low Right: South Korean soldiers in the Demilitarized Zone; Low Far Right: Rock formation, Jeju Island

Page 1—Students in traditional costume celebrate a Confucian ritual; Icon image on spine, Contents page, and throughout: Bowls with bamboo design

Produced through the worldwide resources of the National Geographic Society

John M. Fahey, Jr., *President and Chief Executive Officer*; Gilbert M. Grosvenor, *Chairman of the Board*; Nina D. Hoffman, *Executive Vice President, President of Book Publishing Group*

National Geographic Staff for this Book

Nancy Laties Feresten, *Vice President, Editor-in-Chief of Children's Books*
Bea Jackson, *Director of Design and Illustration*
David M. Seager, *Art Director*
Virginia Koeth, *Project Editor*
Lori Epstein, *Illustrations Editor*
Stacy Gold, Nadia Hughes, *Illustrations Research Editors*
Priyanka Lamichhane, *Assistant Editor*
R. Gary Colbert, *Production Director*
Lewis R. Bassford, *Production Manager*
Maryclare Tracy, Nicole Elliott, *Manufacturing Managers*
Maps, *Mapping Specialists, Ltd.*

Brown Reference Group plc. Staff for this Book

Volume Editor: Sally MacEachern
Designer: Dave Allen
Picture Manager: Clare Newman
Maps: Encompass Graphics
Artwork: Darren Awuah
Index: Ann Barrett
Senior Managing Editor: Tim Cooke
Design Manager: Sarah Williams
Children's Publisher: Anne O'Daly
Editorial Director: Lindsey Lowe

About the Author

TOM JACKSON is a British author specializing in children's books. After graduating with a degree in zoology from Bristol University, he traveled extensively and worked with wildlife conservation projects in Vietnam, Zimbabwe, and the United Kingdom, before becoming a travel writer for a British daily newspaper. To date Tom has written more than 40 books and is a regular contributor to encyclopedias.

About the Consultants

LEONID A. PETROV is a Chair of Korean Studies at the Institute of Political Studies (Sciences Po) in Paris. He is a specialist on the socio-economic history of Korea. Professor Petrov has rich experience, both practical and academic, in North and South Korea. His current research examines the political, economic, and cultural aspects of inter-Korean conflicts and cooperation.

YANGMYUNG KIM is a professor emeritus of political science and international economy at the Academy of Korean Studies, Republic of Korea. His research focuses on international politics, diplomatic history of East Asia, and ongoing information revolution. His publications include *History of the Korean War: 1950–1953* and *Looking Back and Ahead: A Critical Review of Modern and Current Diplomacy of Korea* (co-authored). Professor Kim has made a number of research visits to the United States.

Time Line of
Korean History

B.C.

ca 3000 Settlers from Central Asia arrive in Korea.

ca 900 Farmers from China introduce rice growing to Korea.

108 The Old Chosun dynasty is overthrown by the Chinese Han dynasty.

A.D.

200 The emerging states of Korea adopt Chinese characters for their writing system.

ca 400 Three kingdoms emerge in Korea: Koguryo, Paekche, and Silla. Buddhism is introduced to Korea from China.

668 Silla allies with the Chinese Tang dynasty to conquer Paekche and Koguryo.

676 Silla drives its Chinese allies out of almost the whole peninsula and unites the region under one Korean government, the Unified Silla dynasty.

900s Silla breaks apart in disorder. Many Koreans become Pure Land Buddhists.

936 Wang Kon unifies the Korean kingdoms to create Koryo.

1200

1231–57 Mongols frequently invade the Korean peninsula.

1392 The Yi dynasty takes power and renames the country Choson. It rules from the capital of modern-day Seoul for over 500 years.

1400

1446 King Sejong introduces a phonetic alphabet for Korean to replace the Chinese-based writing system.

1500

1590s Japan invades Korea a number of times under the leadership of Hideyoshi Toyotomi.

1600

1656 Shipwrecked Dutch sailors become the first Europeans to reach Korea.

1800

1876 King Kojong signs the Treaty of Kanghwa, the country's first modern treaty, with Japan to resolve a conflict regarding a supposed Korean attack on a Japanese ship.

1894 A workers' revolt nearly overthrows the Korean government.

1895 Japan defeats China in the Sino-Japanese War and ends Chinese influence in Korea.

1900

1910 An international treaty makes Korea a Japanese colony. The Japanese ban all Korean-language journals and newspapers.

1919 Millions of Koreans protest Japanese rule; Korean politicians establish a provisional government in exile.